SMALL GROUP
ToolBox
GUIDANCE

Ron Kallmier

CONTENTS

INTRODUCTION

There is an old story about prayer with many versions. It goes something like this. There were two farmers who were both praying Christians who had properties on opposite sides of the same hill. At one point of time in the year the first farmer looked at his crop of wheat that was ready for harvest. 'Dear God, please don't let it rain for another two weeks so I can get my wheat harvest in without it being ruined, and then I will have enough to live on for the coming year.' Over the hill, the equally sincere farmer looked at his growing crop of tomatoes and, recognising that without rain the crop would be lost, he prayed earnestly, 'Dear God, please could you send me good rain over the next two weeks so that my crop can ripen, and then I will have enough to live on for the coming year.'

Do you ever wonder how God sorts out our various and sometimes conflicting prayers, whether for guidance, protection or provision? There is a serious level of mystery in this, isn't there? So when we consider our topic we should not be surprised that God has a much broader and deeper perspective than we have regarding even our most simple prayers for His guidance.

When we think of God's guidance a range of images and thoughts may come to our minds. Many Christians seek God's guidance because of specific life situations they are facing – problems that require resolution; decisions that must be made; confusion that requires clarification – these are common situations that lead Christians to turn to God for help.

As important as these reasons are for seeking God's guidance, they can limit God's involvement to the emergencies in our lives and ignore the more significant and transformational goals that God may have in mind for us. When things do not turn out the way we prayed, the real question should *not* be: 'Where was God when I needed His direction?' Rather, we should pause and ask: 'Is my understanding of His guidance too narrow, too limited or too much about me alone?'

We do need to expand our view of guidance to include more than our individual needs and the immediate events and challenges of our lives. There is a bigger story occurring that involves the panoramic plans and activity of God for His creation.

From my personal experience it seems that many Christians celebrate and rejoice in those times when God's guidance has been clear. On the other hand, those periods of silence or uncertainty leave us troubled or confused, causing some of us to question our own faith and perhaps God's love towards us. What may we be missing in these reactions?

We need to keep in mind two important points if we are to avoid a view of God's guidance that is too narrow. The first is that God has a much bigger and longer-term view than our immediate problems, decisions, choices and dilemmas. He has in mind also the wider community of people and world events and not only our little 'world'. The second is that His specific guidance to us always fits within the context of the general guiding principles that we find in the Scriptures.

This study book will explore some of these 'big picture' areas that help us to expand our understanding of guidance. Along the way we consider some suggestions for identifying God's direction in our personal lives. My prayer is that our views of guidance will be stretched in helpful ways and that our sensitivity to God's involvement in our everyday living will be increased.

SETTING THE SCENE

Probably none of us would claim to be an expert when it comes to understanding how God's guidance works in our lives. Like me, you probably have had notable times in your life where God's guidance was unmistakable. Other times may have left you wondering what was going on. Having travelled with God for almost all my life I have discovered a number of basic guidance principles that work for me. These are part of the framework I try to keep in my mind when I come to God for guidance. I trust that they may also be relevant to you in your journey as a follower of Jesus Christ. In its essence, guidance for followers of Jesus Christ is a continuing journey of learning and discovery. What follows are some of the key ingredients of guidance I have discovered on my personal journey.

1. ALIGNMENT

Alignment involves bringing our thoughts and desires into alignment with God's best and higher plans for us (Isa. 55:7–11). To grasp the heart of His guidance we must set our heart, soul, mind and strength to please God and to love God. From the Bible it is clear that God's answers to our prayers are not always what we expect. Humility, love and submission to His loving purposes for us are important foundations for His guidance. In other words, we must align ourselves to His purposes **as a way of life each day**. Then we can be more certain and more comfortable with the directions that He provides.

2. POSITIVE MOTIVES

It is important to check our motivation – that is what drives us to choose a certain option rather than to consider a different direction. This may not be easy to do as some of our motives can be quite deeply hidden, but understanding our real motives is essential if we are to check our alignment. Discovering our true motives can be rather disturbing when we become aware that some may not be as honourable as we would like them to be. Naturally, our motivation will spill over into the way we pray for guidance.

3. TRUST IN GOD'S LOVE FOR US

Often the busyness of our daily lives diminishes our awareness of God's favour and love. Possibly some of our trials are meant to draw our attention back to our God-dependency, and to the incredible truth of His unchanging love for us. The Apostle Paul experienced the best and the worst of times in his journey with Jesus Christ. Out of the extremes of his life experiences he was motivated by the Holy Spirit to pen the assuring words of Romans 8:31–39. His assurance of God's never-failing love kept him strong in the worst of his life's trials.

For those of us who have grown up feeling unworthy or unloved, it is important that we ground ourselves in the same confidence in God's love for us. Without this confidence, it is hard to trust Him to lead us into the very best ways, and to carry us through the very worst of experiences (Matt. 6:33).

4. INCREASING SENSITIVITY TO THE QUIET WHISPERS OF GOD

We may want clear signs for every decision, and the Bible does give us vivid examples where God intervened dramatically and unexpectedly. These unusual events often occurred when God was calling His people to fulfil seemingly impossible tasks. Examples include:

- the call of Moses and the burning bush to bring the Hebrews out of Egypt
- the call of Gideon to defeat the oppressive Midianites
- the announcement to Mary that, as a virgin, she would become the mother of the promised Saviour, Jesus the Christ

On the other hand, it was Elijah who found God not in the dramatic signs but in His still whisper that touched his inner being (1 Kings 19). It is often the same with us.

5. GUIDED BY INNER PEACE – QUIETNESS OF SPIRIT: PHILIPPIANS 4:4–7

For me, this Bible passage is rich with wisdom concerning God's guidance. In fact, it provides an excellent summary for all that has been written above. Especially in trying times of stress or great confusion, it is the awareness of God's peace that can be the certain confirmation of His presence and His direction. When His peace settles in our inner beings, daily issues become clearer and decisions become less perplexing. Often the inexplicable sense of His peace descending on us quietens our stress levels, especially in times of uncertainty or difficulties. The awareness of His peace may be God's means of assuring us that He is leading us in a new direction.

On other occasions His peace may fill our minds, providing us with the confidence to trust Him during the storm we are currently experiencing.

Why not take some time to meditate on these verses included below? Remember that this letter was written by the Apostle Paul when he was a prisoner.

> *Always be full of joy in the Lord. I say it again – rejoice! Let everyone see that you are considerate in all you do. Remember, the Lord is coming soon. Don't worry about anything; instead, pray about everything. Tell God what you need, and thank him for all he has done. Then you will experience God's peace, which exceeds anything we can understand. His peace will guard your hearts and minds as you live in Christ Jesus.*
> (Phil. 4:4–7, NLT)

6. GUIDANCE OFTEN INVOLVES PREPARATION

This brings us to another important understanding about guidance. God's leading today may in fact simply be a preparation, a foundation, for a bigger adventure in the future. When God guided Abram (Abraham) out of Mesopotamia, he never could have imagined how much his willingness to respond to God would change not only his own life, but the history of the world.

7. HIS PRESENCE IS THE KEY

Our awareness that God is always with us brings a confidence that strengthens our hope of guidance (Heb. 13:5–6). For my wife Jeanette and me, this assurance of God's presence has released us at times to make choices. We are free to use our knowledge, experience and reasoning to weigh up the pros and cons involved in a decision we are facing. At the same time we pray to God that He would change our direction if we are heading down the wrong path. This is important at those times when we do not have a clear sense of His leading. Because we have trusted that God is for us, this confidence has given us the freedom to make decisions without the fear of God's displeasure, even when we make one of those inevitable mistakes. We simply try to learn from any false steps and move on, confident that His love for us remains unchanged.

8. EACH ONE IS UNIQUE

Every individual Christian's walk with God is different. He treats each of us as unique individuals and His distinctive interactions with us include how

He chooses to guide us. If we take note of when His guidance is clear we can encourage others with our stories of God's faithfulness towards us. In turn, doing this helps us to grow in our knowledge, confidence and faith as we live in this increasingly unpredictable world (Heb. 10:23–25).

The diagram below provides an outline of how the sections of this study book fit together.

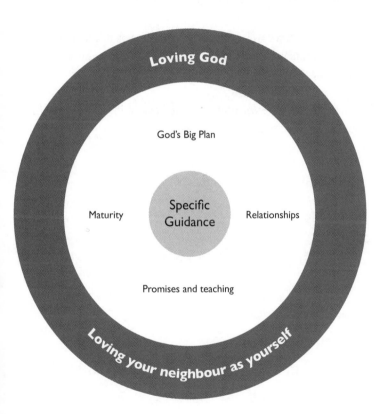

OUTLINE OF THIS BOOK

The sections of this book will help you to explore essential features of God's guidance:

- God's big plan
- The importance of relationships in His guidance
- His desire for our growth towards maturity
- Some specific suggestions about God's guidance for us as individuals

My prayer is that you will enjoy your journey through this study and become more in tune with God's big picture, and more sensitive to the voice of the Holy Spirit in your daily life.

By the way, the CWR Small Group ToolBox book entitled, *Hearing God*, is a companion to this study guide on *Guidance*.

SUGGESTIONS FOR USING THIS STUDY GUIDE

SUGGESTIONS FOR GROUP LEADERS

- As far as possible keep discussions practically orientated, including the Bible study section each week.
- Many of the suggestions for individuals and groups are quite 'meaty' and you may find that you only cover one of these during a group session. This is OK.
- Encourage the group members to do some preparation for the following week. Their best preparation may be as simple as thinking over how they respond to the questions or issues featured in each study.
- For many Christians this is both a fascinating and a confusing topic. From our reading of the Bible we know that God can and does guide individuals, but some of the deeper questions that arise may include:
  'What does God's guidance look like?'
  'How can I be clear when it is God and not just me?'
  'Should I expect God's guidance on the little choices in my life, as well as the big ones?'
- The group times will be the most effective if there is integrity and honesty in the discussion. It is the leader who will be the best example and best encourager in facilitating openness among group participants.
- There are four parts to each of the studies in this book. First, the 'Preview' briefly introduces the set topic and highlights some key Bible verses that help to get readers thinking. Next, 'Personal Exploration' has an individual focus, guiding personal study and reflection. Third, 'Studying Together' provides questions and suggestions for discussing the key Bible passages within a small group context. Finally, 'Applying the Scriptures' raises some thought-provoking questions about practical issues involved in God's guidance today.
- Naturally, you are free to use the suggestions in any way that best fits your own group. While the book is designed to be covered in four small group sessions, you may find it helpful to use some of the suggestions,

discard others and add your own too. Feel free to take as many sessions as are necessary to cover this important topic thoroughly.

- It is recommended that you address **real** questions and **real** issues from within the group whenever this is appropriate. Sessions are not intended to be merely a theoretical discussion, but should be very practical.
- In a healthy group environment, positive experiences and any uncertainties or concerns of group members will surface. This openness will stimulate frank and open exploration of the issues raised.
- Ideally, group members should complete this study series feeling encouraged and having grown in their confidence to discern God's guidance for themselves.
- By the way, we suggest you don't pressure anyone to contribute to the discussion if they appear unwilling. Everyone should be given the opportunity to speak, but also, make space for individuals to process their own thoughts and to consider what is being said by others.

SUGGESTIONS FOR YOUR PERSONAL USE

- This study series aims to apply biblical experiences and teaching to the everyday life experiences of individual Christians.
- In addition to the spaces provided in this study book, you may find it useful to get hold of a small journal or notebook to use while you are focusing on this topic. Here are some things you may like to jot down:
  −Memorable times when you have been aware of God's guidance.
  −Helpful hints concerning guidance that you have learnt from other people or from listening to sermons, reading or viewing Christian teaching or biographies.
  −The main areas where you believe you need God's guidance currently.
  −Any questions and thoughts that arise during this series.

SUGGESTIONS FOR SMALL GROUPS

- If you plan to use the book in a small group, it is recommended that group members all read the 'Preview' section and spend some time in personal preparation for the next group meeting. With our busy lives, this may be quite a challenge but the preparation will help to give maximum benefit to all group members.
- Usually group members find themselves in very different places spiritually when this topic is raised. It is also a topic where individual

Christians may hold quite diverse views because of their background and personal experiences, so it is important that everyone is heard and understood respectfully. Each person's perspective should be appreciated, even when it is not that of other people in the group.

- We can all learn from one another, even from those of us who have serious doubts or questions. Of course, we will need to turn to the Scriptures as our primary authority and source for exploring the history of God's guidance over the centuries.

PART ONE

GUIDANCE AND GOD'S BIG PLAN

 **PREVIEW**

Guidance – the bigger picture

In its essence, the Bible is the record of the unfolding of God's big plan. He has taken into account our human limitations and our failures, but His plan proceeds relentlessly. We are all players in this plan, in a small but not insignificant way.

However, we can so lose ourselves in the demands and struggles of everyday life that we forget that we have a significant role to play in the inevitable and irresistible destiny that God is unfolding in human history. Obsessive self-focus can really cloud this awareness and undermine any divine guidance that we could receive. We may fail to recognise the whisper or the intervention of the Holy Spirit in our lives because our attention and expectation are elsewhere.

General and specific guidance

We each live in our own world of unique challenges and choices. It is essential that we understand that God created us with the power and the privilege to make *some* choices but not *all* the choices we may desire. As we seek to interpret God's guidance we must recognise that there are general principles of guidance that apply to all of us, all the time. These principles become the broad boundaries within which it is safe to make decisions. Take for example a game of football. The outside lines on the playing field are the boundaries for the game. When the ball travels outside that playing area it is out of bounds and the game has to restart within the field of play. There are other rules of the game agreed by the governing body. These are also part of the general guidelines. While the ball is in the field of play and the rules are being followed, the team members are free to make many decisions as a team and as individuals about how they will play the game. Here are **general** guidelines and **specific** choices in operation.

Two of the most important general guiding principles that God has given concerning our life choices are found in Luke 10:25–28. Put simply these general guidelines involve:

- Loving God with all we have and are
- Loving our neighbour as we love ourselves

These principles provide us with a secure safety zone within which we can make godly choices. We can ask ourselves, 'Will this choice express in some way my love for God? Will it help rather than harm others?' Any 'guidance' that directs us outside this safety zone is almost certainly not from God.

These two clear commands remain our framework when we are discerning God's guidance. They provide the ultimate check on our motives. They free us to make our own choices at times or at other times to be responsive to the direct leading of God. By staying within these guidelines, and if we pray concerning decisions ahead, we can confidently make wise choices without the fear that God will reject us, even if we do occasionally get it wrong. This fear that we will somehow short-circuit God's love for us can paralyse our decision-making.

PERSONAL EXPLORATION

1. How often do you take into account God's bigger plan when you are seeking His guidance? Does some adjustment need to be made in your understanding of God's guidance?

2. Take time to reflect on the excellent advice the priest Eli gave to his young helper, Samuel (1 Sam. 3:1–10). Spend time meditating on each of the three parts of this prayer: 'Speak LORD … your servant … is listening'. Invite God to speak to you as you focus on each phrase. Make this your personal prayer.

3. Consider how you can best re-align the activities and concerns of your daily life with the bigger plans of God. Each of us will differ here.

4. From your perspective, does the idea that your life has the potential to contribute to the fulfilment of God's big plan encourage you, amaze you, depress you, inspire you, confuse you, make you curious, or something else altogether?

STUDYING TOGETHER

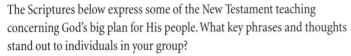

The Scriptures below express some of the New Testament teaching concerning God's big plan for His people. What key phrases and thoughts stand out to individuals in your group?

In Ephesians 2:10 you will observe that God shaped each of us with a unique destiny and special capacities. In each of our lives the Master Craftsman is creating something magnificent. This is true for the most humble as well as the most esteemed among us. We have the pleasure and privilege of discovering how satisfying it is to see God's destiny taking shape in our own lives.

Consider what we learn about God's big plan in one or more of the following passages. What are the key words for members of your group in the passage(s) you select? (It can be helpful to read the Bible selection from a different translation to the one with which you are most familiar.)

1. Ephesians 1:3–14

....

....

....

....

....

2. Colossians 1:15–20

....

....

....

....

....

3. Ephesians 2:4–10

....

....

....

....

....

4. Ephesians 3:1–13

----

5. Revelation 5:1–10

APPLYING THE SCRIPTURES

1. What difference does it make to our attitudes and lifestyle when we are convinced that we have an important part to play in the unfolding of God's big plan?

----

2. When we are locked into an immediate personal decision, what steps can we take to keep the bigger picture in mind?

----

3. Have any of the group members looked back over the years only to discover that God's guidance in a personal matter had in fact a much wider influence or impact (God's big plan) than they could have anticipated?

---

4. If you know each other well, why not take some time to affirm the gifts and abilities that each person in your group has been given by God. This can assist each of you to recognise more clearly your part in God's big plan. You may like to record below any comments made to you.

---

5. From the Bible or from the lives of people you know, can you recall examples of personal guidance clearly meshing with God's big plan?

PART TWO

GUIDANCE AND MATURITY

 ## PREVIEW

It may be surprising to find **maturity** here in a discussion of God's guidance. However if we consider the passages below (and many others) we find that God is extremely interested in our individual growth towards inner maturity. We can expect that His guidance will have greater maturity as part of its goal. It is worth noting that growing towards maturity and growing in wisdom run hand in hand. James 3:17–18 gives us a very helpful picture of wisdom. We would expect to find these same qualities in a mature Christian. We will look at James 3 in more detail in one of the reflection exercises to come.

From the example of Jesus in Luke 2:41–52 we learn that true maturity touches all we are (especially verse 52). For example, it is possible for an individual to be a superb athlete and yet abusive in their relationships and in a mess emotionally. It is essential that we recognise that God's guidance is for the *whole of life*, and not just specific episodes when we feel 'stuck' or threatened or confused. The best life foundation we can have for expecting and experiencing God's guidance is for our Christian faith to be active in every part of our daily lives, and not just the parts we may consider 'religious'. Jesus certainly lived this way. In the Gospel of John (chapters 5–8), Jesus Christ describes Himself as a Person who:

- Always ought to please the Father
- Only did what He saw the Father doing
- Only said what the Father was saying
- Always did the work of His Father

He is our ultimate example of this *whole of life* commitment. As we read the Gospels, it becomes clear how in touch with His Heavenly Father's guidance He was.

The Bible stories show us that there are times when God's guidance does break through into the lives of those who are not walking in His way. As disciples of Jesus, however, we have the privilege of seeking His wisdom continually, simply because we are God's children. In its essence, discipleship is about us choosing to follow where Jesus is leading 24/7. If we have a life committed to pleasing the Father and the Son we will become more aware of the promptings of the Holy Spirit.

God's guidance, for me, has been more of a gradual unfolding and not a total blueprint for the years ahead. Looking back over many decades, I see His hand at work on many occasions. What has surprised me is that what seemed at the time to be relatively minor pieces of guidance actually shifted the whole direction of my life. For example, when I was a very young man, I remember sitting outside my family home one day after coming home from the school where I was a teacher. I was praying for guidance as I tried to decide whether to undertake a university undergraduate programme at night, or to learn a musical instrument. Thankfully for all those people with a musical appreciation and gifting, I was accepted onto the university course. Unknown to me at the time, this was the doorway to many years of study, and shaped the nature of my Christian ministry and life history so far. What appeared to be a rather simple decision at the time was, in fact, a critical event in my life. God always has the big picture of our lives in view. We do not and we cannot.

Keeping this point in mind can really help us when God allows us to go through those tough times we all face. Joseph is the classic example of this. Sure, he was unwise with his words as a young man and that helped to undo him. After decades of appalling treatment by his family and others, however, he came to see how God used even the painful times to bring him to maturity as a spiritually astute and highly competent national leader (see Gen. 50:15–21 – especially verse 20).

Certainly we may grow through successes and victories, but often the trials provide the fire to forge purity of spirit and maturity of personality if only we are open to exploring what we can learn in these seasons. No experience is wasted under God's hand if we allow Him to work all things for good and for His purposes. God may not cause our troubles but He certainly can use them.

PERSONAL EXPLORATION

1. God's agenda can be worked out even in those events that are intended to be harmful or hurtful to us. He works irresistibly for our good. Consider the significance of Romans 8:28–30 in any tough times you are experiencing.

2. Take time to undertake a personal stocktake of your growth towards maturity in Christ over recent years (or months if you are a new believer). Consider the following areas: spiritual life; thought life; choices; emotional life; relationships; physical wellbeing.
   You may find it helpful to undertake this following exercise prayerfully. This is not an exercise designed to discourage you if you uncover weak areas. We all have them. Rather, self-examination can help you find God's direction in those weak areas for your development. It will be even more helpful if you can work on this activity with one or two trusted friends so you can encourage and support each other.

   Areas where I have grown

   Areas where I may be stuck

Areas where I seem to have slipped back

_____

_____

_____

_____

Future growth areas

_____

_____

_____

_____

STUDYING TOGETHER

1. Psalm 23

   Revisit this familiar psalm, considering it from the point of view of God's guidance. The psalm covers some of the best and the worst that life can throw at us. What do you discover? Do you find anything in this psalm that provides clues about how to have a successful journey through life?

   _____

   _____

   _____

   _____

2. James 3:13–18

   We noted above that a mature person can be recognised partly by their wisdom. Explore the difference between false wisdom and true wisdom as found in these verses. How can these positive wisdom qualities influence the way we pray for guidance?

   _____

   _____

   _____

   _____

   _____

3. Hebrews 5:11–14

There are some interesting comments here regarding the signs of mature believers. What stands out to you? What do you discover about how to grow in maturity as a Christian?

-----

4. Ephesians 4:11–16

Maturity is not only God's desire for individuals, but also for groups of Christians together. On occasions His guidance will be designed to increase the harmony and maturity within a Christian group. What qualities may God desire to bring to greater maturity in a group like yours?

APPLYING THE SCRIPTURES

1. If one of the goals of God's guidance is our personal maturity as individuals, how will this fact change the way you look at the trials and difficulties that come your way?

-----

2. Maturity involves body, mind, soul and spirit. In Western cultures the emphasis has been very much on body image and, to a lesser degree, on the mind. What can be some of the consequences of inadequate attention to the development of the soul and spirit?

_____

_____

_____

_____

_____

3. Think of someone you respect (past or present) who shows a holistic maturity. What qualities do you see that make you regard them as a mature person?

_____

_____

_____

_____

_____

4. Some people say, 'I don't ever want to go through that again, but I value what I learnt from the experience.' Looking back on some hard times in your past, how did God use these experiences to make you stronger, wiser or more mature?

_____

_____

_____

_____

_____

PART THREE

GUIDANCE AND RELATIONSHIPS

 PREVIEW

Previously we considered the two broad boundaries on our choices. These were: loving God and loving others as we love ourselves. Love of God, healthy love of self, and love of others are essential components of this dynamic mixture. There are strong relational themes in these commands. One way of describing the nature of this love is that it is *committed to the best interests of the other person(s)*. Selfishness can certainly derail guidance.

From the Genesis account of creation we discover that from the very beginning God planned to enter relationship with human beings (chapter 2). At the same time, by creating people, God also made possible all types of human relationships – friends, family and so on. It is essential that we recognise that there is a dynamic connection between our relationship with God and our relationship with each other. Failure in one type of relationship contaminates the other type of relationship. Genesis chapter 3 gives us the first example of this in action. Some of the greatest challenges that come our way are to do with relationship problems. We can be confident therefore, that God's guidance will have healthy relationships in mind.

RELATIONSHIP WITH GOD

A number of Christians whom I know appear to receive accurate and specific guidance. These people have made pursuing God's presence a high priority. Seeking His face is not so much about **our posture** (kneeling, lying down and so on) or **our petitions** as it is about our awareness of **His Presence** (Psa. 27:4–14).

We can learn much from the parable of the prodigal son in Luke 15:11–32. This son did not value the relationship with his father. He saw his father as a means to an end and used and abused the family relationship and its privileges. He was manipulative, embarrassing, shameful and extremely selfish. In his culture, by demanding his inheritance as he did he implied that he thought his dad was taking too long to die.

The older brother was no better. He may have stayed at home but his self-interest is there for all to see. It is shameful for us today if we treat our Heavenly Father only as a means to an end. No relationship deserves that.

The Lord's Prayer gives us a perfect example of how to avoid this selfish focus without ignoring our very real personal needs (Matt. 6:9–13; Luke 11:2–4). The first focus of this prayer is on God – His glory, His kingdom and His will. The prayer then shifts to our needs and our failures. Finally it addresses our need for God's protection. What a great framework this provides for our prayers.

With this in mind, have you ever thought of beginning your day with a prayer for guidance that goes something like this: 'Heavenly Father, I worship You and want to please You. What are You doing today that You want me to be involved in? I am available, so please lead me. I trust You to provide for me today and care for my future needs.'

RELATIONSHIP WITH OTHERS

Have you been aware of times when the Holy Spirit brings people or situations to your attention? This awareness may come through something external – a phone call, a comment from a friend, a photo on your phone, or in some other way. There may be other times when a name simply pops into your mind, seemingly out of nowhere. Your attention becomes focused on the person or situation. You may wonder what this means? Is it God or is it just your memory being fired up by something around you? Perhaps it is God's way of prompting you to take some action. If you are unsure about whether it is God or not, simply ask Him to show you. Get on with life and see what happens next. If the thought persists you may make contact in a casual way to see how the person is. 'I've been thinking of you during the last day or two and I was wondering how you were doing?' If it is a situation that gains your attention, perhaps prayer is the obvious response.

It can be surprising how God leads us to contact a person at just the right time. Let's never forget that He is full of love for His children. In responding to this prompting, you may find that you become God's answer to another person's prayers (Heb. 4:16).

PERSONAL EXPLORATION

Below are a selection of psalms to guide your thinking in this whole area of guidance and relationships. You may prefer to look at the entire psalm.

1. Psalm 27:4–14

   This psalm is a beautifully expressed and balanced prayer from the heart of David. It centres on his relationship with God. Which words inspire you? Which words encourage you?

   ----

2. Psalm 25:1–7

   Why not begin meditation on this psalm by asking God to focus your attention on words or verses that are important for you to understand right now. This is certainly a psalm about guidance, but its focus is very much on God.

   ----

3. Psalm 31:1–5,14–20

   This whole psalm is a deep prayer from the heart of David, for safety and guidance (verse 3) in a time of deep distress. What do you discover in this psalm that can assist you in your own prayers when you are going through a particularly tough time?

   ----

4. **Psalm 133**

   This psalm has an unmistakable Hebrew flavour to it, yet it captures God's continuing passion for unity. What benefits flow when our relationships are harmonious?

STUDYING TOGETHER

1. **2 Corinthians 5:16–21**

   The heartbeat of God is filled with a passion for reconciliation with us, no matter how far we may have gone from Him or how often we live our lives ignoring Him. This reconciliation also brings us into alignment with God's guidance in a deeper way. Do you find any ideas here that are very relevant to you right now?

   ------

2. **John 16:12–15**

   When we read the Gospel accounts of Jesus' relationship with His disciples we notice the affection and care He had for them. This care and affection continues, unchanged, towards us today. What did Jesus promise for all disciples concerning wisdom and guidance? Note down any thoughts that are particularly important for you at this time.

   ------

3. Colossians 3:12–17

   The wisdom found in these verses is relevant for all Christians throughout the history of the Church. Maintaining healthy relationships is a central theme in these writings of the Apostle Paul. Which of his instructions may be especially challenging for Christians today?

   ---

4. Acts 4:32–37

   The whole of Acts 4 is stirring and challenging. What desirable qualities and actions flowed from the deep unity among the believers in the early Church? Do they appear to have been especially sensitive to one another, and to God? Why do you think this was so? What can we learn from their experience today?

APPLYING THE SCRIPTURES

1. Do you agree that God has the strengthening of our relationships in mind when He guides us? Is this a helpful concept for you? Discuss your ideas.

   ---

2. If a sincere Christian is about to pursue a course of action that he/she believes is guided by God but appears to you to be unhelpful, or maybe harmful to others, how could you approach the person?

3. We understand that none of us are perfect and that maintaining good relationships with one another is hard work. What should be the balance between prayer and action when relationships break down among Christians?

4. What part do Christians have in helping one another to discern how God is guiding them? Explain your point of view concerning how this works in practice.

PART FOUR

GUIDANCE AND DIRECTION

 PREVIEW

It is important to trust God's general promises, but how do we gain specific guidance for our unique decisions? I have added some suggestions below from my own experience for you to consider. They are in no particular order.

- Get to know the Scriptures as well as you are able. God uses them to stir your inner being (spirit) and prompt you in a particular direction.

- Learn from the journey of other Christians in this area of guidance. What do you discover from their experiences?

- Faith in God is a feature of spiritual maturity and often it has an essential part to play in our guidance. Be prepared to step out into the unknown if necessary. God occasionally (often?) pushes us outside our comfort zones.

- Open doors can on occasions be a very positive sign of His guidance, especially if a door opens unexpectedly. God's provision of the resources you need is another way He brings confirmation.

- Sometimes we may have an inexplicable inner sense of 'rightness' – a certainty in our spirits that this is the way to go, but yet the way ahead appears blocked (a closed door). This is where the teaching of Jesus in Luke 11:9–10 applies. Sometimes we have to persist. The skill is recognising the difference between a permanent closed door and one that needs some pushing.

- There are occasions when dreams form a part of God's guidance. Of course dreams may have a purely psychological basis, yet God certainly does use dreams to guide us at times. It is wise to ask for further confirmation before proceeding in a particular direction based on dreams alone.

- Similarly God may use prophetic words from others to guide us. From personal experience, some prophecies we have received have been profoundly accurate and life changing. A word of caution – any human involvement can easily be tainted, so prophecy is more compelling if it comes from people who do not know us or who do not know our situation. Again, further confirmation is advisable with prophetic words.

- Be willing to approach important decisions using your experience and reasoning, when necessary. This may mean using a notebook to record every positive and negative reason for and against the course of action you are considering. Prayerfully lay the list before God, asking for His peace, and then make your decision confidently.

- Wherever possible discuss big decisions with people you trust. This is essential if they are involved in the decision or its effects. Often they will have a perspective that you may not have considered. They can be more objective than you.

- Make a note of occasions when God's guidance has been clear. How did that guidance come? What did you learn from the experience? Learn also from your own personal decisions. What worked? What did not go so well? Would you do the same thing again?

- When your decision involves a number of attractive options it is essential to bring God into the decision. He will see things that you do not. Look for His peace in your final choice. We have found that it may not be the most obvious option.

- From the opposite perspective, we sometimes have to make a choice in situations where all the options appear to be unappealing or negative. Prayer and the advice of trusted people, added to some clear thinking on your part, are important at these times.

- *When in doubt don't do it!* If you feel uncomfortable about a choice or direction you have in mind it is best to wait until you have time for further consideration, advice and/or prayer. Being cautious can prevent regrets in the future.

Would you change or subtract any from this list? From your knowledge and experience would you want to add to this list?

The diagram below attempts to explain some of the factors that have influenced our assurance of God's guidance over the years.

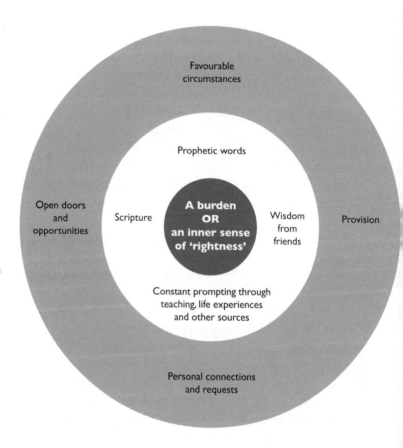

PERSONAL EXPLORATION

Why we seek guidance

1. Which circumstances present the greatest challenges for you when you seek God's guidance? How do you reach decisions in these types of situations?

2. Are you ever aware of something deeper within you – some underlying, powerful emotion, attitude or motivation that must be considered and dealt with before you can be free to make the wisest decisions? Examples would include things like: anger, hopelessness, inadequacy, self-protection. Dominant issues such as these will cloud your judgment. If you recognise any similar things in yourself, what steps could you take to overcome them?

3. A healthy degree of self-knowledge is a valuable asset in decision-making. It helps us to know what is within our present capability and what is not. Let's not forget that God may want to extend our present capability or move us into new areas of activity. Has this been part of your experience?

4. Have people you know told memorable stories of God's guidance? What were the main factors that convinced these people that the leading was from God? Did you gain any valuable insights from their experiences?

_____

_____

_____

_____

_____

STUDYING TOGETHER

The early Church had to start from scratch. They had no background for discerning God's leading in this new era of the Holy Spirit. Despite this, the Holy Spirit was able to lead them to achieve incredible, world-changing things. It is reassuring to know that God is still at work, directing and encouraging His people on all continents today. Also, in recent decades, stories of the remarkable activities of God are becoming ever more accessible through electronic media. He continues to lead the poor, the disempowered, the uneducated, as well as those who enjoy many advantages. He speaks to people from diverse cultures and countries. He continues to lead new believers and seasoned veterans of the faith into many faith adventures. Their stories are a rich resource for those of us studying guidance.

We turn now to some events in the Book of Acts. This book contains a variety of examples of God's guidance. Here we discover the beginnings of this amazing faith journey where new Christians began walking in step with their Heavenly Father through the Holy Spirit's guidance and power. What do the selections below reveal about the methods God used to guide His people?

1. Acts 9:10–19
   Ananias and the conversion of Saul

_____

_____

_____

_____

2. Acts 13:1–3
   Paul and Barnabas set aside for apostolic ministry

3. Acts 15:1–21
   The council of elders in Jerusalem

4. Acts 16:1–15
   The call to Macedonia

5. Acts 18:24–28
   Priscilla and Aquila in Corinth with Apollos

APPLYING THE SCRIPTURES

1. Mary was so right when she said to the servants at the wedding in Cana, 'Do whatever he tells you' (John 2:5). This is also excellent advice for you and me today. Are any group members aware of times when either they did or did not respond to the quiet promptings of the Holy Spirit? What was the outcome and what did they learn from that experience?

2. As this series draws to a close, it may be appropriate to take time to discuss any other practical approaches individuals in the group use to make decisions.

3. What important decisions are group members facing at present? Invite individuals to share about their situations. This should be a practical opportunity to support one another and encourage each other.

4. It is recommended that you close the final group session on this topic with prayer for one another. If group members have particular needs for wisdom and guidance, bring these before God.

FINAL COMMENTS

God's guidance is a serious matter. He leads us because He loves us and because He has important things for us to experience and to achieve. Once we are clear on God's direction for us we are obliged to respond to Him with a resounding, 'Yes, Lord!'

In the Gospels we find two accounts of the central teachings of Jesus. The first, found in Matthew chapters 5–7, is commonly known as the Sermon on the Mount. The second is sometimes called the Sermon on the Plain. It is found in Luke 6:17–49. Significantly both these parallel sermons end with a story of two builders. Seriously consider the implications of Luke 6:46–49 as you bring this study on *Guidance* to a close.

APPENDIX: BIBLE PROMISES AND TEACHING ABOUT GUIDANCE

Relevant selections from the Scriptures can become a rich source of meditation and guidance in our lives. A number of Christians I know have one or two passages of Scripture that have been impressed on their hearts and minds many times over the years. These have become a foundation of confidence and comfort through their life journey. Of course it is possible to take unwise, random selections of verses out of context, believing that they represent God's specific guidance. Sadly, through the years people have done this very thing and the results have occasionally been unhappy, confusing and even harmful. Ultimately it is the work of the Holy Spirit to impress upon us those passages and promises of God that are particularly relevant to us.

Despite this potential problem, the Scriptures themselves affirm their own value as a source of God's guidance. Below is listed a selection of Bible passages that do this. It is suggested that you spend time considering each one, asking God to reveal to you in what ways the written words are relevant to you. Consider especially the key words you notice in each selection.

- Psalm 119:105
- 2 Timothy 3:14–17
- 2 Peter 1:19–21
- James 1:22–25

On the next page is a selection of familiar passages that are important when we consider God's leading. It may be helpful for the group to prepare a list of the main ideas from each passage. From your discoveries, which do you consider to be the most difficult of these truths to keep in mind when you require God's specific guidance? Which are easier? Consider the reasons for your choices.

- John 16:1–15 (The ministry of the Holy Spirit our Counsellor – the source of guidance)
- Proverbs 3:5–6 (Devotion to and trust in God – the basis of confidence in His guidance)
- Hebrews 13:6–8 (A promise of God's continual presence and closeness – our Guide and our Friend)
- Matthew 6:25–34 (The promise of God's provision for his children)

When applying the Scriptures personally we need to keep a number of things in mind:

- the whole passage rather than simply an individual verse or two, perhaps taken out of context
- the context (historical moment) in which they were given
- the people to whom they were originally given
- the reason the words were spoken or written
- the reason why we believe the promises are still relevant to us today

You may like to use these pages to journal your thoughts as you explore how God leads and guides you.